BUOYANCY
And Other Myths

ALSO BY RICHARD PEABODY

Poetry
Sad Fashions
Echt & Ersatz
I'm in Love with the Morton Salt Girl

Fiction
Paraffin Days

As Editor
Coming to Terms: A Literary Response to Abortion (w/Lucinda Ebersole)
Mondo Marilyn (w/Lucinda Ebersole)
Mondo Elvis (w/Lucinda Ebersole)
Mondo Barbie (w/Lucinda Ebersole)
Mavericks: Nine Independent Publishers
D.C. Magazines: A Literary Retrospective

BUOYANCY
And Other Myths

Richard Peabody

GUT PUNCH PRESS
Cabin John, Maryland

For Rachael, my mother

Some of these poems have previously appeared in the following places: *Abbey, Bogg, Carolina Connection, Dancing Shadow Review, G.W. Review, Kansas Quarterly, Lithic Review, Night Music, Nightsun, The Pearl, Pittsburgh Quarterly, Plum Review, Pocket Lint, Poet Lore, Potomac Review, Ruby, Slant, Sotweed Review, Taos Review, Union Street Review, Uno Mas,* and the *Wayne Literary Review.*

First Edition

Copyright © 1995, by Richard Myers Peabody
All Rights Reserved

ISBN: 0-945144-06-7

Library of Congress
Cataloging in Publication No.: 94-78592

Cover photo: "Midsummer's Night Dream," by Toni Frissell, taken December 1947 for a *Harper's Bazaar* fashion editorial. Photo courtesy Frissell Collection, Library of Congress.

Special thanks to Derrick Hsu for his excellent suggestions, and to the Virginia Center for the Creative Arts for the terrific stay and the chance to write many of these poems. Plus thanks to Jim Williamson for the good eye, Nita Congress for the printer, and to Ann Acosta, Herman Ayayo, Jamie Brown, Jane Fox, Beth Harper, Judith House, the late Ken Louden, Liz Murawski, Rebecca Nagle, Susan Nickens, Paul Pasquarella, David Sheridan, and Zenon Slawinski for keeping me active in the work force.

Typeset by Barbara Shaw, Bethesda, Maryland
Printed by McNaughton & Gunn, Saline, Michigan

Gut Punch Press
P.O. Box 105
Cabin John, MD 20818

"The biology of purpose
keeps my nose above the surface."
— Brian Eno

"Walking on water
wasn't built in a day."
— Jack Kerouac

CONTENTS

I. Shooting Myself in the Foot
Family Secrets   11
Pickers   13
Safe As Houses   15
The Forgiveness Device   17
My Grandmother Always Told Me   19
One Night in Juarez   21
Passing the Thunderbird   24
Carolyn   25
Beginning, Boundary, End   26
Goodbye, All My Fathers   28

II. Kissing Games
Cor Anglais   33
Dating Vampirella   34
Guitar Player   36
She Discovers Jazz   37
The Other Man is Always French   38
Strictly Confidential   41
Attachment Hunger   42
Isle of Dreams   44
Chaplin Dans Limelight   45
A Miserable Pile of Secrets   47
The Sound of Wings   50
As Bees in Honey Drown   51
One Less Red Town   52

III. Between Funerals
I Live Behind a Bakery   55
Winter Panacea   57
Women, Fire and Dangerous Things   58

Orbits   59
Football Hell   61
What's Your Favorite Toxic Smell?   62
Burning the Dolls   63
Ain't No Big Deal   64
Unfinished Business   66
Sounding the Territory   67
Overtaken By Events   69
Cranes   70

Shooting Myself in the Foot

Family Secrets

1.

In the brother dream,
I've got him by the throat
shaking sense into his skinny neck.
Music isn't enough tonight.
Scratching, clawing, eyes like stones.
If I erase him I will expand.
His sins wiped clean. Nowhere
for him to leer from. No perch
or receptacle that can hold that
peculiar weight. He gives up.
Yet I'm still not satisfied. He always
gives up. And I want to shake him and
say don't give up. For God's sake
don't give up again. Hit him
with my guitar. Drive sense into
him. Then I wake up and he's gone.

2.

Father has a new boat.
He likes to ride on top of life.
To be in it and on top of it.
The boat never goes backwards.
And father never looks back.
That's taken me a long time
to figure out. Me so busy
looking back. Him always
two steps ahead of me.

3.

Mother believes plaster
can cover all the cracks
and little hurts. And it does
for a time. She's short-sighted.
Plaster is good enough for her.
Except that I think long-term.
I want things to be okay.
To settle like cider
after it's swirled.
All the particles to the bottom.
She thinks I'm missing the point.
That the cracks are gone.
Oh mother, the cracks will
always be there. Always.
Just beneath the surface.

Pickers

Those mystery women
who pulled the feathers
from dead birds
were always round
and full of laughter.
Nothing like the jagged
maids who cared for me
when my mother had to work
the summer months.

They usually lived in shacks.
Junk cars rusting next to
tarpaper outhouses. Chickens
littered about the yard. Mangy
dogs underfoot, who barked
at our white skin.

My father would heft
the day's kill out of
the car trunk, each body
loaded down like a beanbag
from all the shot.

Almost flirting,
the women would
laugh and carry on.
Making broad gestures.

Their men taking
a drink from a bottle,
while the children
walked up to examine
the shiny car.

I could no more imagine
their lives than I could
comprehend plucking
all those feathers.
No amount of money
could possibly have
been enough.

Somewhere in that shack
where dogs lay tongue-wagging
in the shade there had
to be a gigantic freezer—
the secret of the profession—
stocked with food
meant for other mouths.

A specific magic
for long lines
of hunters who left
their bloody gifts.

Safe As Houses

My brother and sister and I played prairie dog
when we were kids. We'd watched them
on Disney and later at the zoo.
We set up chairs with blankets and pillows
plus an old Ken-L Ration barrel
from my father's pet shop.
Then we'd imagine tunnels and roll
around in the dark for hours.

I used to read under the blankets
with a flashlight and dream about
tunneling through my bedroom wall
in the basement and building
my own secret room connected
by hidden passageways.

Yet in real life I've always been
afraid of tunnels. Have visualized
the one across Baltimore Harbor
collapsing like Moses' Red Sea
a hundred times...
and I can't believe
they've actually drilled a tunnel
through the ocean floor
to connect England and France.
What are they thinking?
One earthquake and well...

What I guess I'm trying to say
is that I'd rather think about
prairie dogs and children's games
than deal with images
of giant U.S. Army bulldozers

covering thousands of shell-shocked
Iraqi soldiers under an ocean of sand.

Any mine cave-in or capsized ship
seems like just another disaster film
compared to those doomed men
watching that tidal wave
roll right over them.

Imagine sand...
clogging every orifice—eyes-ears-nose-throat.
That moment of recognition
knowing you're trapped
in Edgar Allan Poe horror
and buried alive.

The Forgiveness Device

"Hold that flashlight still."

But I can't. It's impossible.
I'm only a child and I watch
as he puffs up bigger and bigger
—like a barrage balloon—
pushing back his glasses
that are smeared with grease
as he winds the clicking
ratchet again and again
changing sparkplugs in the dark.

The garage light won't reach outside
to where we stand around the
burgundy Chrysler. I'm scared.
Snot dripping down my face. Tears.
The fender is too big for me
to lean over, but I try
and my arm is so numb
it tingles. The drop light
flickers against the hood.
My father is stripping skin
off his knuckles as the ratchet
slips and dings off the manifold.
He's talking to himself.
Saying he can't see and
beginning to cuss.

I realize now—
that he's angry at himself,
at his failure to fix
something so elementary
and his anger

is misdirected at me.
But back then I was just
a bookish little kid
afraid of failing.
I didn't know yet that
it's okay to fail.
That my father was
just trying to save a buck
and afraid of aging.
The price was high.

Why can't you wait till morning?
I wanted to say, but didn't dare.
He drinks another Ballantine,
crumples the can and drops
it on the driveway.

If I could
I'd materialize at that exact moment
the aluminum still rattling
against the concrete.
Tell him, "It's not that important Dad.
It's just a couple of sparkplugs.
Don't get so stressed."
I'd rub my red bandanna
across his forehead
and soothe his brow.
Tell him, "Relax."
And watch his features soften.
Hear that laughter again.

And I'd forgive him.
I really would.

My Grandmother Always Told Me

I should be
a minister

perhaps
I've missed
my calling

up on stage
every Sunday
hands raised to heaven

each new congregation
rallying round my
fire and brimstone
sermonizing

riding
from parish to parish
like some evangelical
Paul Revere

actually the nomadic
lifestyle
appeals to me

stripped down to basics
and on the go

each year
brings a new town
new dwelling

maybe my grandmother's right

I still remember
the ministers
from my early churchgoing days

a voice
like a hammer
falling

another who
sent me postcards
from Africa

a strong handshake
after the service
or funny glasses

and always,
always,
indelible eyes

One Night in Juarez

The border crossing cost two cents
and you walked across the bridge to Mexico.
The muddy trickle of water below was the
Rio Grande but it didn't
look like it does in the movies
and you didn't feel any different.
It was already dark and small boys
dressed in white stood shrieking
like emaciated ghosts on the concrete banks
of the great sewer so American
tourists would toss them coins.

You felt sick confronted by the ragged army
of beggars, some with patches over
empty eye sockets, others with crippled
legs or empty sleeves. All with the
inevitable outstretched hand saying
"please-please," as if it were the
only English word they knew, hoping that
some good Samaritan from the north
could still be moved by pity so they could
buy a shot of cheap tequila before they slept.

Now even the bald-headed guy
with the plaid shorts and Instamatic
knew you couldn't be a good Samaritan
to a few million people and like him
you closed your eyes and your heart
and kept on walking, past the tiny boy
bloated and dead, who cursed you
when you finally stopped to check.

Off you went past the taxi-cab drivers,
the tourist traps, the pimps and whores,
until unable to cope with the degradation
you fled inside the nearest doorway
through a dark passage lined with doors
which emptied finally into a garish bar
where a loud jukebox played the latest songs.

You hadn't even sat down and
a brown-eyed girl of sixteen
had her hand down your pants
asking huskily if you'd like to "fuck-fuck."
It didn't matter if you went or not
for some soldier from Fort Bliss
would pop through the door and take her
if you didn't, so you laughed
and bought a bottle of tequila with the worm
and drank until the filth inside
the bar was knee-deep
and just as foul as the filth outside.

Only then did you begin to understand
what America has done with its dream of money.
You tried to explain this to a whore's
white-haired father who was crying on your
shoulder, begging you with choked sobs
to tell him about the United States
that legendary El Dorado where the
streets were really paved with gold.

But you couldn't lie anymore and told him
that we didn't have the answer either,
even though you knew this ancient Coronado
wasn't paying any attention, only listening
to his dreams, still hoping you might be
drunk enough to fuck his daughter
so he could buy another drink.

At dawn, with the laughter of whores
still ringing in your drunken ears,
you crossed the bridge to El Paso
certain of what you'd find there,
sick at heart that it wasn't something more.

Passing the Thunderbird

When I was at Ohio University
my roommate from Detroit and his crew
would do almost anything to get high.

They drank NyQuil, put toothpaste
on cigarettes and smoked them,
made gangster punch—the key
ingrediant a can of
pineapple juice added
to a bucket full of everything
else in the liquor store.

One day they brought home
an elephant tranquilizer.
You know, the kind they
shoot into a bull elephant
with a high-powered rifle.

I can still see Killer and Bubbles
slicing it into four parts.
Dennis holding up what
looked like a piece of chalk, saying,
"Hey Rick, this piece is for you."

Bubbles slapped my *Electric Ladyland*
album on the stereo and I remember
thinking that if everybody loved
Hendrix as much as the four of us
that somehow the future would be all right.

Carolyn

There are times when I hear her voice. Times when
like Abraham I'd give my son to hear the right thing.
To hear that she'd survived. That she was moving in
next door. That I'd get to see her, if only in
passing, like watching some anonymous actress on the
screen, knowing that she can never be real
because beautiful or black and white. The memories
are skimpy, as underdeveloped as the baby rabbits
caught in the lawnmower blades when I was little.
And when I think of them, clenched, pink and tiny,
I think of her, huddled in the wreckage, her limbs
molded into the body of the car. For a month
afterwards I replayed the scene where we'd last talked
and blamed myself for not having the guts to ask
her out though I had two tickets for a show. As though
going out with me would have changed everything.
I repeated her name over and over after I heard,
like a litany to memorize that face, until I played
the tape out, and the face was no more. The scenes are
gone. Melted into the memory of a memory. I'm left
with nothing but her name, which I carve on doors
in the winter when it is so cold I know nothing
that matters can live anymore.

Beginning, Boundary, End

"This was almost your mother,"
my father said, pointing out
a photo in his wallet
of a young woman in uniform.

I can't recall her name—
some insubstantial Polly
or Anita. No doubt retired
with grandchildren by now.

How my mother felt about
that photo, I can only guess.
After all my father had kept
it as a memento. I'm still
too young to know the code
concerning such things.
Must one abandon all such
relics? Vestiges of pre-
connubial bliss? Is that
what commitment means?

After his death I wanted
to salvage the photo.
I don't know why exactly.
That leggy young woman
was important to me,
that's all. A part of my
father's world I know
next to nothing about.
Before wife and family
anchored him in the known.

Don't kids always assume
their parents were childhood
sweethearts? They rarely
entertain other possibilities—
father might have been quite
the man about town, or mother
the small town heartbreaker.
One never really knows.

Goodbye, All My Fathers

My father was always larger than life.
You could think *Stagecoach* era
John Wayne and capture him about right.
The Hemingway hero made flesh.

He's so young on the screen.
More agile than I remember.
And handsome too. Much more handsome
than the other hunters or guides,
juggling admiration and envy as they
carried his kill from the launch
a frame or two earlier. And this
strikes me odd. Because I never
noticed when he was alive.
Never thought about him that way.
Yet, he wears a red lumberjack
shirt like a champion.

Such a puzzle, a father. Dead now,
three years. His voice reverberating
in my skull the instant I think of him.
Each time I think of him.

When I called his friends to tell
of his passing, some wept, did their
level best to comfort, or told
anecdotes to me the eldest son,
the one anointed "Junior," though
I could never live up to the name.

To some he was a real hero.
A man of action like Duke Wayne,
the idol of his own dark Saturday
matinee imaginings. A role model.

One friend told me he felt like
a "paper shuffler" by comparison.

Hard for me to believe
a man like that could ever die.
I keep rewinding the film
like a voyeur. I would have
been about twelve then.
Believing he was god
for another year or two
before racing into total rebellion.

Until I realize with a start
that we're now exactly the same age
existing simultaneously
through the miracle of video.

He was the man who had everything,
in his prime, in Newfoundland
on a mythic hunting trip with
his cronies, a business back in DC,
plus a wife and three kids.

And yet I know he was disappointed
that the moose had just stood there.
No sport at all. Like shooting an
elephant. But that's for me in
retrospect. On screen, in
that time, in that place, my father
was a force of nature—my indoor
life as tame as the milk I add to my tea.

I've never been to Newfoundland.
And sitting here in my cramped apartment

—sans wife, kids, and business—
I'm awestruck that he could have
had everything I want that young.

You wouldn't think he had a care in
the world. One look in those clear
blue eyes and you almost believe it's true.

Kissing Games

Cor Anglais

No amount of money
can top the way
you catch me in your eyes.

No patronage award,
or tenure job
will do.

My NEA grant
is in the way
your voice turns
me inside out,

wraps me in splendor
like a white fan
of pearls.

Dating Vampirella

You've always wanted
hungry kisses
and boy howdy
these are hungry
with a capital H.

She's a vampire
with a difference
all right.

The black high heel boots
are a bit out of date
but the red cutaway
catsuit still works.

She doesn't need
to use her mesmerism
you're hooked.

Eventually you learn about
the daily blood substitute
Planet Drakulon
and her penchant
for handcuffs.

The sex is incredible
and you're safe and sound
as long as the plasma
doesn't run out.

Then one day
watching her change
into a bat and fly around

loses its appeal
and you're bored.

Tired of playing Robin
to her blood sucking Batman.

So you devise a game.
"Vampy, come quick,
I cut myself."

She hesitates
but licks the wound clean.

So you say,
"What would you do
if I smashed all
the plasma?"

Vampirella smiles.
The real adventure
is just beginning.

Guitar Player

Fingers know secrets
that eyes can't understand.

She Discovers Jazz

stumbles over it
     more likely

purloined letters

as though love
is spelled

Wynton

and jazz
something
that never existed

your records
invisible
all those years

a moon
whose gravity
she refused to obey

until his ears

more interesting
than yours

heard

what she
was trying
to say

The Other Man is Always French

The other woman can be
a blonde or a redhead
but the other man
is always French.

He dresses better
than I ever will.

He can picnic
and stroll
with a wineglass
in one upraised hand.

Munch pate,
drink espresso,
and tempt with
ashy kisses.

He hangs out
at Dupont Circle
because the trees
remind him of Paris.

Did I mention sex?

Face it—
he's had centuries
of practice.

I'm an American.
What do I know?

He drives a fast car,
and can brood like
nobody's business,
while I sit home
watching ESPN.

He's tall and
chats about art—
I don't even want
to discuss that accent.

He's Mr. Attitude.

My fantasy is to call
the State Department
and have him deported.

Only he'll probably
convince you to marry him
for a green card.

No way I'm going to win—
the other man is
always more aggressive,
always more attentive.

The other man
is just too French
for words.

From now on
I'm going out
with statuesque German women

so next time we run
into each other
they can kick his butt
for me.

Strictly Confidential

Pigalle lights
blink off

tired neon.

Ann's in bed
kicking one
exquisite leg.

"Are you thinking
of minks or Cadillacs?"

"Both."

Never tell
a woman anything.

"What you told
in bed,

she told
in bed."

Bob the gambler
has crapped out.

"Where shall
we go?"

"The Carpeaux
of course."

Ann cups
perfect hands.

"Give me
the moon."

Attachment Hunger

I've dropped
into some nether world
where Dionne Warwick
songs really matter.

"Walk On By" and
"Say A Little Prayer."

I want
fresh angels,
skin machines
glittering in sawdust.

"Anyone who
had a heart."

I can't keep
from crying.

Even la Belle
Dame sans Merci
grows weary.

Leaves
in search of accents
uncircumcised delights.

We say love
and want telepathy,
shared secrets,
flesh magnets.

"Promises, Promises."

"You may never
get to heaven
if you break my heart."

It's possible.

And here
on dark avenue

emotions
in dire need
of grounding

"no words
of consolation"
matter.

Isle of Dreams

The rejected lover knows
he must finally give in
and change the sheets,
knows at 3a.m.
on a rainy Tuesday
—the bed really as
hard as she always claimed—
that she's never
coming back to rest
and that it's useless
to pretend any longer.

And in that beautiful
moment—before
gathering up the past
and clutching it to
his sunken chest—
leans over her pillowcase
one last time, inhales
deeply, smiles, and thinks
"Cantaloupe Island."

Chaplin Dans Limelight

If I drop your hand—

Do you drift
celestial
out of my line of sight,
lost weather balloon,
Amelia Earhart.

Or simply,
out of reach—
another country,
a different state of mind.

I am tethered
by my cane,
your parasol,
the old soft-shoe.

Don't let go—

Let's cakewalk
into town,
eyes closed,
kite tails
tangled
perilously.

If I'm messy—
you're hopelessly elegant.

Your bonnet
and upturned leg,
potent shadows
on my wall.

I'm always looking back—

Too serious
in my moustache
and strawboater,
afraid,

pebbles on
a distant shore.

Don't let go—

Not now—

Even if you fall
I'll raise you up.

Oh how we dance.

A Miserable Pile of Secrets

So I'm watching a lot
of Little League baseball
in my new home town.

Another relationship gone bust.

And I'm enjoying the kids.
Many are one-time patients.
When I start hearing rumors
through the grapevine
about the new Doc.

I ignore this of course,
figure it'll blow over.
Only it begins to get worse,
more obvious at the games.

So I know it's sexist,
but I ask the trashiest nurse
in the entire hospital
to go to a game.

And she's thrilled,
chewing gum and
wearing Spandex,
there's a lot of body contact
and the more beer she drinks
the louder she gets.

I can feel every eye on me.
When Candi wanders off to
the ladies' room again
a man surprises the hell out of me.
He puts out a beefy hand and says,

"I want to apologize Doc.
I was wrong about you."

"How's that?" and I go
all goofy grin.

I am determined
to play the rube now.

"Well, ahh…
let's just say
I was worried about you."

"Worried about what?"

He's not stupid.
He's beginning to
get the picture.

"You're all right Doc.
Let's just leave it at that.
Me and the Missus"—and he
gestures a couple of rows
up to his ponderous
Republican wife—
"We're real glad you're—"

"Hi Dale. Is your back okay?"
Candi stops him cold.

He jumps about a foot,
mumbles something and
awkwardly makes tracks.

"There are more secrets
in this small town
than you'll ever know,"
Candi says, and smiles
as if to say, "I know
why you chose me."

She puts both arms
around my neck to
maintain her balance
and I put a hungry arm around
her waist to maintain my own.

The Sound of Wings

You know they're folded up tight
underneath that black leather.
And wish tonight you were the one
crossing the bedroom to help unfold them.

You undo the leather thongs
and release rare beauty,
unwrap the gauze and
guide them gently into place.

The streetlights and
venetian blinds brush
stripes across her feathers.

She's smiling now—
feel the draft
as she exercises
those first tentative motions.

After making love you drowse—
she keeps you cool
by beating her wings.

As Bees in Honey Drown

There's still honey in your voice
when you answer her unpredictable
late night phonecalls.

A sympathetic counterpoint
to her breathy whispers.

She has always been able
to make you quiver.

And don't think
your new lover
hasn't noticed.

If a voice could give life
perhaps this is the wavelength
it might choose.

Burnished sweet as clover honey
—that split-second hesitation
before sliding over the lip
of the jar—folding back onto
itself in golden ribbons.

One Less Red Town

the little black dress
is very sad

you never take it
out any more

Between Funerals

I Live Behind a Bakery

And watch the sky turn
Tar Heel blue above the
red brick every morning.

This big ventilator fan
sticking up in the air,
sending all sorts of
glorious smells my way.

Henry Miller
would have loved this place.
He called bread
"the Staff of Life."

I'm always stocking up on loaves.
Raisin-Walnut, Pumpernickle, Sour Dough.
I don't eat them fast enough.
My Rye turns ergot.

There are times I wish
I could make something
as substantial and necessary
as this stuff
I fold into my mouth.

I've never baked bread in my life
and now I want to learn.
Like the fantasy sequence
in *Castle Keep*,
a World War II film,
where Peter Falk becomes a baker.
My shaping mechanism
wants to knead and knead
until something new is created.

Only most days
it's easier
to just read a book
with that smell
all around me
and think buttery thoughts.

Winter Panacea

Sometimes a parrot
becomes necessary.

A Picasso.

A robe
for our discontent.

Today's snowfall
as sluggish
as gin.

Women, Fire and Dangerous Things

Yes, of course she's responsible,
fire born in root beer breath,
to sizzle now in pine needle
and eel grass.

She studies flames,
chocolate eyes
moist with possibility.
Fire trucks in the foreground
drawn like magnets from every precinct.

Outlaws rage across horizons,
unruly, wild, out of her control.
She's not worried though.
Smoking cigs with girlfriends
at school tomorrow, she'll
play the authority and squeeze
every drop from this adventure.

Orbits

Life is like a picaresque novel.
Sooner or later everybody returns.

The guy you dissed in shop class
now a motorcycle cop writing out
a very special speeding ticket.

That cute student you never called
hanging on the arm of your arch rival.

Time and space don't alter the pattern.
Most orbits concentric or elliptical,
crashing into your life with the regularity
of the seasons—after days, weeks, months.
Others, parabolic like comets, can take years.

Your best friend's kid sister
announces a decade old crush.

The high school girlfriend
you didn't ask to the prom
finally forgives you
seventeen years later.

They all come back.

The unrequited love who ignored
a dozen long stem red roses
arrives at the fancy dress party.

The drummer institutionalized
for ingesting too much acid confesses
he always hated your guitar playing.

This week's guest stars wait in the wings.
The doorbell is ringing.
Also the telephone.

"You can see them or where they're going
but not both at the same time," your
unobtainable rogue star goddess says,
materializing to find you
pinned on your back in the middle
of the red Native American carpet
like a stray bit of Skylab.

"Don't panic. It will end in time."
She laughs. Nudges your legs
with a sequinned black slingback.

You wish you believed her.
How on earth did you get so jaded?

No sweet hyperbolae
as far as the eye can see.

Football Hell

Imagine
spending your
entire college
football career
without winning
a game.

Some players
make a joke of
the losing streak.
Pretend to be proud
of the tradition.

Once they're
on Wall Street
the futility
will be history.

It could be worse.

Not like the
perennial doormat
of the Ivy League
was Catawba or Ball State
where the future
might be running
a dry cleaning
shop

and living
it down.

What's Your Favorite Toxic Smell?

Some people like turpentine.
And while I'll admit to a
true love for spray paint
(I can always be counted on
to glue scale models together)
and strong infatuation with gasoline
(Oh that's okay honey,
let me pump it this time),
right now,
hovering over the kitchen sink
the heady smell of chlorine
is what my German blood craves—
mixing Clorox and ammonia
like it was the most natural thing in the world.
Wondering why swimming pools
aren't fatal to small children.
Or do we, like mosquitoes,
just grow immune as we get older?
My head aches and the room is
doing your basic stutter dance.
Ahh this is the life—
my cups are whiter,
my sink is brighter.
I have this friend
who puts herself to sleep
every night by painting
the inside of her head white.
When she says this I imagine
tiny robot cartoon brushes.
My way is so much easier.
The chlorine dances
and so do I.

Burning the Dolls

Not really hate, or some demento girl-boy thing.
Just curiosity and being around them day-in, day-out,
scattered across my sister's lily-white dresser.
And having moved on naturally from zapping
ants with a magnifying glass, to disfiguring
toy soldiers with a woodburning kit, and still further
to torching model airplanes, the dolls were simply
the next logical step, since we couldn't buy flamethrowers.

We dragged Barbie, Ken, Skipper and Midge, along
with Chatty Cathy and anybody else we could find
out into the backyard, stripped them down, positioned
them provocatively astride each other, doused them
with lighter fluid and had a plastic bonfire.
The results kind of reminded me of a Vincent Price
film—*House of Wax*. Torsos melting one way,
limbs another, heads imploding like smashed pumpkins.

The smoke was black, green and gray. Perfect
preparation for what would happen during wartime.

Ain't No Big Deal

You could see her coming
a mile away.
Pink cowboy boots,
pink bag,
blue jeans and blonde hair.
She was a bit
out of place
in Northwest
moving fast
up Wisconsin Avenue
swinging that bag
to propell her skinny frame.

She might have just
had a bad night. Or been
out for a Sunday stroll.

I was stunned
by the pink,
by her drop dead
good looks and
six foot frame.

She moved like a cheetah—
as lithe and willowy as that—
and when she paused,
reached a hand up the
crack of her ass
and looked right at me
I almost died.

I wasn't sure it had
happened at all.

She took off without
a second glance
and I watched her
disappear
up the hill
by channel 9.

A week later I was on
14th street en route to
a gig at Javarama
when she came running
straight at me
her makeup a little
worse for wear.

No bag, no boots, no pink.
She was strangely barefoot
and wore an olive tanktop.

She might have had a fight.
I thought about chasing her,
to find out what was going on.

But it seemed
like more *trouble*
than it was worth.

Unfinished Business

A large man sits down
next to you on the bus.

"I kill cats for a living,"
he says, avoiding your eyes.

You, too, have killed cats.
Put their boxable shapes
in cardboard and set them
afloat. Waited for permeation,
for silence.

The man presents one hand
and then another. They
are *big*, abrasive,
even for blood sports.
Hands large enough to smother
a nest of squirming birds.
Basketball hands, meathooks.

You press your right hand
into his, muscle down
until the fingers firmly lock.

Sounding the Territory

For years it was a sense of place
you most wanted. Home was not enough.
So you sat in diners nursing coffee,
explored caverns, climbed mountains,
and were never content.

Your place as distant as ever.
Something you couldn't squeeze
in your fist, or tack posters
on, and move into.

Your passage was erased
just as quickly in Taos as Hatteras.
Sand conspiring against a non-fossil.
A flashlight with dead batteries.

It's not immortality you're after.
What then? A safe harbor?
A sense of belonging?
A location you could sink your feet in.
Wet cement. Grafitti. The endless poems.

In school you wanted to be liked, needed,
and admired. To fit in. To have people trust
your opinions, listen to your ideas,
make you feel important, and give you
a reason for living.

Left home forgotten
like a wet raincoat.

Books stashed in attics to mildew.
This book mildewing.

A place one can crawl back into,
like dreams, like rats coming
to the dump night after night
when they know people are waiting
to shoot them.

A place to feel at home.
Your own turf.
Where you're in charge.
Where every free parking space
has your name on it and
nobody else knows the short cuts.

Where you're safe and sound
and everything works.

Overtaken By Events

I am no longer
surprised
by atrocities.

I'm surprised
that anyone
else can be.

I am no longer
surprised
by cruelty

bone orchards

killing machines

scorched earth.

They have become
a way of life.

Nobody
will be born innocent
in my lifetime.

There is
no such thing
as a little
atrocity.

Atrocities
have become
as familiar
as words.

Your words.

My words.

Cranes

slash the sky
like gallows
for giants